# "TOMORROW," MY SISTER SAID; TOMORROW, NEVER CAME

# "TOMORROW," MY SISTER SAID; TOMORROW, NEVER CAME

Metha Parisien Bercier

Copyedited by Michelle Pam Fabugais
Reviewed by Kimberly Joyce Veloso
Book Illustration and Photography by Veronica Vallie Mercer
(Grand Daughter of the author)

Library of Congress Control Number:        2013902262
ISBN:            Hardcover                978-1-4797-8443-1
                 Softcover                978-1-4797-8442-4
                 Ebook                    978-1-4797-8444-8

This book was printed in the United States of America.

**To order additional copies of this book, contact:**
Xlibris Corporation
1-888-795-4274
www.Xlibris.com
Orders@Xlibris.com
125318

# CONTENTS

# PART THREE

# ACKNOWLEDGMENT

To my husband, children, grandchildren, and great-grandchildren for their patience and understanding in allowing me time to write this book.

To my parents; my sisters, Helene and Lucy; and my brother Tommy, for kindling the sparks to remember.

To all my loved ones who have since passed, may you rest in peace.

I Love You All!

# PREFACE

When I first thought of writing about my life experiences at an Indian boarding school, I had only to search the archives of my inner mind, where there, neatly tucked away, were the olden thoughts and memories of my childhood school days.

After discarding the dust and cobwebs that had collected through the years, I paged through those early chapters of my life and found them to be as vivid as when they happened. A little blurred, perhaps, yet well enough to take me back in time.

# FOREWORD

When the Europeans first ventured into the great Northwest Territories of Canada, they found various Indian tribes occupying this vast tract of land. These first explorers were mainly of French origin. They cohabitated with the Indian women, mainly the Cree and Chippewa tribes, and in a short time, a new race of people evolved.

Endowed with one-half Indian blood and one-half European blood, they called themselves Le Metis, a French term meaning "one with mixed blood."

These Metis people multiplied very rapidly. Unlike their full-blood brothers, they quickly utilized the best of the Indian heritage and the best of the white man and incorporated this knowledge into a new culture, a new language, a new race of people.

As much as I can recall, my great-great-grandfather was Hyacinth Parisien, who married Josette Carriere. They had two sons. Ignatius Parisien, the younger, married Margarett Letendre. Her parents were Louis Letendre and Marie Hallett. The eldest son, Jerome, married Justine Gladue. These two became my grandparents. From this great union came my father, John Syril, who married my mother, Rose Elise McGillis.

The McGillis name goes back to Scotland. According to my family tree, Donald Ban Mor McGillis, United Empire Loyalist, was born in 1730 in Muneraghie, Inverness-shire, Scotland. He married Mary McDonnell, daughter of Ronald McDonnell of Lundie, Scotland. They came to the United States and settled in Tryon County, New York, where one of their sons, Angus McGillis, was born. As a young man, Angus ventured into

Canada and worked as a clerk for the Northwest Company and also for the Hudson Bay Company. He later settled at St. Francois Xavier, Manitoba, Canada, in 1824. Angus married Marguerite Notinikaban De Bout. This was the start of my Metis ancestry.

The hereditary aspect of the Metis people is much intermixed. In most families, the progeny is deeply evident. In the Metis heritage, one may see both dark—and fair-skinned offsprings, a beautiful race of people.

The language is very impressive and unique. It was easy to understand because words were composed of French, Cree, and Chippewa in the same sentence. Very few spoke the full-blooded Indian language, and then some spoke fluent French. The Metis language is a very direct language. Much could be said and understood in one word. The dialect and accent were very much French. No amount of government schooling could erase this hereditary trait from its people; it is here to stay.

Very little history has been written about the Metis and their vast accomplishments. Credit was always given to the white man or to the full-blooded Indians. The Metis were never accepted in either the white society or totally by their Indian brothers. The differences were too many. When all the land was taken from the Indians and the Metis, they were forced to live on reservations. Many came south from Canada into Montana and into the eastern part of North Dakota to place their roots once more. A six-by-twelve-mile reservation was set aside for the thousands of Indians and Metis people who were at one time masters of the plains, waters, and mountains to settle on.

Here they still live in what is considered the poorest land in the state of North Dakota, chosen by the United States government for them to etch out a livelihood, to survive if they could, and to continue to dream the impossible dreams of yesteryears.

It has been a very slow process, a process that still has a long crooked road to travel. Yet in spite of this upsetting turmoil of hardships, sorrows, and pretentious joy, we still have everlasting hope.

We did survive, and we will continue to survive. We may yet prove to our captors that a true native of this land never dies and is forever embedded with time. Each day of life, we sense him treading softly with the seasons, reminding us that somewhere amid the mountains, plains, and valleys, the echo of his footsteps lingers on and on.

# EDUCATION

In 1819, a law was passed that authorized the president to employ capable persons to instruct adult Indians in the field of agriculture and the children in reading, writing, and arithmetic.

For almost fifty years, various religious orders conducted Indian education on the reservations. In 1876, a new policy was adopted. It was structured under strict government auspices. "Indians must be civilized,"[1] they said. "How can they exist with their customs in the midst of civilized society?"

Who determines what civilization is the right one? I ask. Don't even the animals, birds, and all living creatures upon this earth have their own civilization? If we were an uncivilized people, why, I ask, did they eat our foods, use our medicines, steal our inventions, and copy our constitutional way of life? Why are they still searching for and questioning the wonderment of the Indian culture? And yet they condemned us. "The Indians must be separated from all traditions and customs, and he must be stimulated by a perverse and more invigorating social and moral atmosphere. If we want to humanize, Christianize, and educate the Indian, we should endeavor to divorce him from his primitive habits and customs. The Indian is the strangest compound of individualism and socialism run to seed. It is this being that we endeavor to make a member of a new social order." Condemning further, they said, "We must re-create him! Make a new personality!"

---

[1] Quotations taken from *Indians at Work*, a newsletter from the Office of Indian Affairs, Washington, DC.

And so the roundup was in full force. "Catch those young Indians, separate them from their parents! Teach them the white man's way!" From all over the country, thousands of little Indian boys and girls were rounded up and shipped hundreds of miles away to government boarding schools to be re-created and humanized.

These children were forbidden to speak their native language and were severely punished if they did. Parents were subjected to corporal punishment if they objected. The young were made to understand that all that was before was wrong.

And so it was written: governmental commandments for all Indians to abide by. A governmental bible that reeked of totalitarianism, of minds who felt above the Creator. *How daring is stupidity!*

It was during this era that my two sisters and I were suddenly thrown into this unknown world. Three long years of unknown time, eternal time for children as young as we were. Each day stretched into another endless day, each night for tears to fall. *"TOMORROW," MY SISTER SAID. TOMORROW NEVER CAME.*

# PART ONE

# MY BEGINNING

I was born in the Turtle Mountain Chippewa Indian Reservation on August 6, 1922, in Belcourt, North Dakota. My father had built a one-room log cabin among the foothills by Saint Michael's Catholic Church near Belcourt, North Dakota.

It was here that I first became aware of life and the lives of my close-knit family. My parents are of Chippewa, Cree, Scotch, and French heritage. The language spoken at home and throughout the reservation was a mixture of Indian, French, and English, which came to be known as Metis. The English language was used very sparingly. The dialect was predominately French, and our parents spoke to us using such.

My parents had been married ten years. Seven children had already been born into this union. A number that was increased to eighteen as time went by. The eldest child was Helene, and then came Lucy, whom we called Be Boos. Then my brother Tommy was born, then me. Two younger sisters and a baby brother followed. Ours was a happy home filled with love, laughter, song, and dance—and *KIDS*!

Over the rise of a large hill lived our beloved grandma. A short distance to the right of her home lived our young cousins.

We lived a secluded life, rarely going anywhere or visiting with other people. We were content living a simple life amid the wonders of Mother Nature. *This was our world, the only one we knew.*

# STRANGE VISITORS

It was a very hot autumn day in August 1927 when my brother Tommy came bursting into the house, screaming, "*Ae'n-shar! Ae'n-shar!*" (a car, a car) as he pointed toward the bend of the old dirt road.

"*Mon dieu, mon dieu,*" (my goodness, my goodness) answered Mama, making her way to the door. Putting her hands to her face to shield it from the glaring sun, she strained her eyes to make out whose car that might be.

Turning quickly, she excitedly told us in our native tongue that it was the men from the agency. "Hide, hide in the bushes," she quickly ordered. Confused, we scampered to the side of the house where the chokecherry bushes were thick. Peeking through the foliage, we got a glimpse of the two men stepping out of the car. "Those are the police," Tommy whispered. "I know that's how they dress."

The two men were peculiarly dressed. Both wore baggy knee pants with black high-top boots and flat little caps on their head. Glancing toward the house, we saw Mama standing in the doorway, carrying the baby, while our two little sisters clutched closely to her side.

The men began talking to Mama and then entered our house. We continued to hide in the thickness of the bushes, very still while quietly staring at each other in suspense.

"I wonder what they want," whispered Tommy. "If only Papa was here!" Cautiously, he crept to the edge of the bushes to get a better view.

"Don't try anything!" whispered Helene. "What are you thinking?"

"Well," whispered Tommy, "Papa told me I'm the boss when he's gone."

"Huh?" whispered Helene. "That's what you think."

"Shhh-sh, they're coming out," Be Boos whispered.

Pushing the tree branches away for a better look, we saw the two men walk to their car and drive away. Still scared, we got up, making sure the car took the bend on the road as we raced toward the house.

Mama was sitting on the bed, carrying the baby, and looking very sad. "Mama, what's wrong?" asked Helene.

Fighting back her tears, Mama began to tell us why those strangers were here. Helene, Be-Boos, and I were going far away to school in two weeks.

"Where?" asked Helene.

Fighting back more tears, Mama said, "Well, somewhere. A school. You'll have to go, or the police will come to see Papa, and we won't get any help from them if you don't go!"

"Tommy too?" asked Be Boos.

"No, no!" cried Mama. "I didn't tell them about your brother. I hope they don't find out. The three of you will be together. Tommy would be alone with strange boys," she said, crying louder.

The conversation was confusing to me, yet I understood enough to know I was going somewhere. I started to jump up and down and clap my hands with excitement.

"Look at her, she doesn't know what's happening," quipped Helene.

"I know she'll cry, maybe she shouldn't go . . . she's too small," said Mama.

"She will be an old lady when she comes home," laughed Tommy. Holding up three fingers in front of my face, he said, "This many years you'll be gone!"

How much was that? I thought. Was it a long while or a short while? I didn't care! Hearing the news didn't have much of a meaning to me. I was going someplace, and that was enough to make me overly happy.

When Papa came home from work that night, Mama told him the sad news. Setting his lunch pail on the table, he slowly sat down on a chair. Reaching into his pocket, he pulled out his tobacco and made himself a smoke. As Papa stared into space, I went to stand by him and hugged his arm. Turning, he looked at me and smiled.

Papa was old; his whiskers were long, and I could see the dust embedded in them. A sorrowful look seemed to cover his entire face. Then showing the kindest smile as he always did, he put his arms around me and said, "So you're going away to school? School will be good for you. You'll get smart. You won't have to work hard like me for a living." Laughingly he added, "You won't get tired and dirty like me. Oh yeah, they have good food, nice beds to sleep on, clean clothes. Maybe for a little while you'll be lonesome, but you'll be all right, you'll see." Again, that feeling of excitement seemed to flow over me.

# PREPARATION

I remember Mama being very busy the following days. Mama made each of us a pretty cotton dress. She also sewed underslips and bloomers made from bleached flour sacks. I noticed she was being especially caring and loving until a sudden sadness seemed to cloud her eyes.

Papa came home from work one day and brought each of us a hand-me-down coat. Some caring friend had heard of our leaving and offered to help. Mine was a pretty red one with a furry collar that had a little face at one end. I didn't like it! I didn't want that little head with the beady eyes so close to my face.

As the days sped by, the time drew nearer. Mama was hugging and kissing us more than usual. I remember my brother Tommy wanting to be much closer to us too. Tommy, the little leader, was suddenly letting me do what I wanted. Everything I asked to do was fine with him. One day, I wanted to go to our favorite spot, the tall hill. We had gone there so many times before to lie on our backs just to stare at the sky. And so now, we were up there once more. Our best friend, the sun, was looking down at us.

"You see that sun up there?" he suddenly asked me, pointing with his little finger. I glanced up; it was so big and bright and warm. "Papa said he's the boss of the world. Papa said when people are good and work hard, the sun gets big and shiny all day. But if people are bad, he cries. That's when it rains."

I believed him completely. After all, Tommy was older than I, and I sensed he knew much more than I did. He was always by Papa's side, and Papa could do anything and everything. I felt that my papa was the smartest and strongest papa around. And Tommy shared his knowledge very proudly, as often as he could to the rest of us.

Tommy was the one who showed me where turtles laid their eggs. One time, we found fifteen or twenty eggs buried in the ground. "See!" He pointed. "These turtle eggs have no shells. They're not like chicken eggs." Another time when walking through the woods, he showed me where little squirrels hid their supply of wild hazelnuts for the winter. "Right here," he said, again pointing to the old dead trunk of the tree that was partly hidden in the ground.

My brother was so smart. He knew so much. One time, we were picking berries, and my legs touched poison ivy and burned so badly. He quickly plastered mud on my legs, which prevented me from getting a rash. And if by chance you did get a sore from the ivy, he would make our dog lick the infection until our skin turned a pale color, a process that never left scars.

"Did you know that some ants have wings?" he asked. You don't believe me, do you? Well, I'll show you," he knowingly said. A few days later, some ants landed on the kitchen table, and he was quick to point out his previous knowledge. "See!" he said excitedly. "These are piss ants, see their wings?"

Tommy told me never to kill moths too. He said they ate mosquitoes. He was wise for his age. He was my best friend. He was the best teacher I ever had.

I was to remember all this down through the years. It was an education of sorts that one does not learn in school. It was learning through experiences, learning through the senses, the smell, the touch, and the hearing that made a complete cycle of the immediate knowledge that one's mind craved for. How great are Mother Nature and all that it contains. No book has ever been written that is older or more knowledgeable than this great gift from God. "Respect every living creature, everything that grows, for you see, we never know what mysteries that they contain," said Papa. "So as long as you keep your ears and eyes open, you can't forget," he added. And forget we never did.

We raced back down the hill and found Mama packing our small belongings in a brown paper bag. "When are they leaving?" asked Tommy.

"Two more days, the past two weeks went by so fast," Mama answered.

The next evening, Mama made us a special dinner and a big homemade cake. Papa sat at one end of the table and Mama on the other end. We kids lined the sides, standing as we ate, and listened to what Papa and Mama had to say. I remember Papa telling us to always be good girls and to say our prayers each night and morning.

"Come here, all of you," he said. He sat me on his lap and hugged Helene and Lucy closely. We loved being close to Papa. He was so big and strong and so very kind and gentle to all of us. He turned to Helene and said, "Now you, Helene, you're eight years old." And you, Be Boos, you're seven. And this one, she's only five. I want both of you to take good care of her. You will have to take Mama's place until you come home again!" He turned me sideways on his lap and teasingly said, "Now don't you go and get too fat, or you'll look like that water barrel outside." He laughed!

As young as I was, I remember sensing something that I couldn't fully understand. My mind was ejecting only excitement, eagerness, and anticipation! It made me feel so happy.

According to my sisters, I was a rather plump, attractive little girl with large dark eyes and olive skin. I had a bubbly personality and loved to sing and dance the Charleston or the Red River Jig that Papa and Mama had taught us.

Once more, Papa played his fiddle; and Helene, Be Boos, and I danced for the last time.

# DAY OF DEPARTURE

"My girl, get up. It's time to get ready." I opened my eyes and saw Mama bending over me. "Shh," she whispered, "don't wake the baby." My aunt Madeliene was sitting at the table, sipping coffee. She was going to watch the little ones for the day.

Mama helped me dress. On went my new homemade bloomers, underslip, and then my new dress. I was so excited! Mama thought it was sort of a chilly morning and decided we should wear our new coats. "I don't like my coat," I said as I softly sobbed. Mama held it up for me. "It's pretty, put it on." Reluctantly, I did.

Papa had already cranked up the Model T Ford, which was sputtering with loud noises. "Well," said Papa, "are you all ready to go?" Mama put her hat and coat on and told us to kiss everyone good-bye, which we did very quietly as to not wake the little ones. Once outside, Aunt Madeliene gave each of us a few pennies to buy candy. "Well, kiss your brother, and we'll have to get going," said Papa. Tommy gave each of us a quick hug and turned quickly to stand on the small wooden platform in front of the house. As we began to drive away, I looked back at Tommy with his patched blue overalls, barefoot, shading his eyes from the sun with one hand, and waving good-bye with the other. Good-bye I waved, not knowing that we wouldn't be back for three long years.

I remember our old Model T Ford chugging along strange roads and different scenery. After some time, we approached a small settlement where we stopped.

Papa went into the small building and came out carrying a few items. He handed each of us a small bag of peppermint candy. I gasped with delight! Never had I had so much candy to myself. I clutched the little bag tightly, for I was not about to let it out of my sight.

As we continued along, I noticed everyone was unusually quiet. At times, a few sniffles came from Mama. In the distance loomed two tall buildings. "We're almost there," said Papa. "I don't think we're late." In a few minutes, we drove up to a long dark-red building where people were gathered around in small groups.

"See that over there," said Papa. "That's the train you'll ride on." I stared, thinking, *Why are all the houses stuck together?* We all got off the car and walked over to where the people were. As I stood there clinging to my papa's hand, I was startled by a loud, clanging sound. Papa looked at us and said, "Well, it's time, I guess." Bewildered, we walked toward the train.

A tall man was standing on a small platform, calling out names. And then he said, "Helene, Lucy, Metha."

Mama muffled more sounds as she pulled us close to her. Holding us tightly, she brokenly whispered, "My little girls . . . I'm going to miss you so much!" Very perplexed, I wanted to cry. I didn't like seeing my mama cry.

The tall man helped us onto the train. I turned around. Why were Mama and Papa still standing there? *Why aren't they coming too?* I thought. As the man guided us inside, we were all told to sit. I tried looking out the window, hoping to see my mama and papa. Helene pulled me back. "Shhh, sit still," she cautioned me. More people came in. I looked desperately again, trying to see Mama and Papa. Suddenly, we heard the clanging and loud whistle and slowly the train began to move.

Once more, I got up and pressed my face to the window. "Mama, Papa!" I cried until their faces faded in the far distance.

I sat there between my sisters, very bewildered and confused. I looked around and saw other children my age and some much older. All were sitting quietly, staring into space. My sister must have sensed my disturbed state of mind as she put her arm around me and pulled me close to her.

I was getting a little uneasy; it was too quiet, so I slid down below the seat and sat on the floor. I noticed there were cracks down there, and I could plainly see the rails and board planks as we sped along. Reaching into my pocket, I found the pennies Aunt Madeliene had given me. One by one, I dropped them through the openings, trying to hit the boards down below. "Whatcha doing?" whispered Helene as she pulled me up and told me to sit still beside her.

A man passed by, carrying a box of candy and Cracker Jacks. "Five cents," he hollered. I wanted some, so Be Boos bought me a box. Excitedly, I spilled my Cracker Jacks all over the seat, trying to get at the little toy I knew was inside. My sisters looked annoyed, yet neither said a word.

Suddenly, I had to go to the bathroom, but where? My sisters didn't know either. Remembering, I pointed to the cracks on the floor. "Go fast!" Helene whispered in our native language as she gave me a slight shove downward. Crouching between my sisters, I did what I had to do without a care. Pulling me up again, Helene told me to sit still between them. I sat there with a jumbled mind, staring into emptiness.

I must have dozed off to sleep for a while when suddenly, a loud, long, lonesome sound startled me. I sat up quickly. That was the same sound I heard when I last saw Mama and Papa. A man walked down the aisle and told us to get ready to change trains. Coming to a halt, the man motioned for all of us to follow him to the door.

Once outside, we were directed to stand in line until further notice. My sisters held on to my hands tightly. "Are we going home now?" I asked Be Boos. She shook her head no. The urge to cry came quickly. She studied me a moment and annoyingly said, "Don't cry!" I muffled my sobs and clung to her tightly.

Just then, a man walked up to us and told us to follow him to another train. Once more, we were grouped together. Inside the train, I noticed we were in a much nicer room. The seats were softer, and there were no cracks on the floor. Once again, we were on our way. I squeezed my way to sit by the window. I noticed we were moving swiftly. I also noticed men working in the fields and cattle grazing in meadows. I glanced downward and thought to myself, *I know I could jump down there.* Tommy and I would wrap ourselves in old green army blankets and roll down the tall hill, and we never got hurt. I also noticed the sun was slowly setting.

A lonely feeling engulfed me. I couldn't hold back my tears. I wanted to go home. I wanted the world I had known. I wanted my mama. I wanted my papa. The more my sisters Helene and Lucy tried to console me, the harder I cried. "Shhh," Helene whispered. As I closed my heavy eyes and lay my head on her lap, I heard her softly say, "Tomorrow . . . tomorrow, we'll go home."

# DESTINATION

Helene was shaking me. "Metha, wake up. We have to go." I sat up and noticed bright little lights above us. Everyone was standing and gathering up their belongings. Again, the tall man yelled loudly, "Pick up your things and get in line. You are to get off the train and follow each other to the large truck outside. Do not get out of line."

Quickly, Helene and Be Boos picked up our belongings then shoved me between them as we made our way out the train door. Following the group, we came to a large canvas-covered truck. A man lifted us in turns into the dark interior. We were ordered to sit on the floor and keep quiet. After a short, bouncy ride, the truck stopped. Another man was there to help us get off the truck.

I looked around in wonderment. There were tall lights and big, big houses all over the place. A strange-looking, heavyset woman wearing a blue dress with a white collar and cuffs was standing at the curb. "Follow me," she said in a loud, stern voice. My sisters held my hand as we followed the group along.

Once inside the building, the woman led us to a very large room where dozens of strangers from other reservations were being directed as to what they should do. Standing tall and stately, she glanced over at our newly arrived group several times. Then her eyes seemed to rest on my sisters and me. I stood there, staring in wonderment at the strangers, the huge room with the high ceiling, the strange muttering of the ones in charge. Walking very briskly, the woman came up to where we were standing and said, "Are you sisters?"

"Yes," replied Helene.

"Uh-huh," the woman said, nodding her head. "Separate them!" she ordered to one of the officers as they began to push Helene in one direction and Be Boos in another.

"Helene," I cried as I made a dash to her side. I was quickly pushed back across the room. "Where's my sisters?" I cried.

"Hush!" the woman snapped back at me.

"I want to go home," I cried again, thinking she could understand me.

In a loud, shrill tone of voice, she continued to talk and use arm movements so that we could understand her better. I still continued to cry, only to be pushed along with other strange little girls into an outer room. There we were told to take our coats and shoes off. "Pile them here," she ordered. Tearfully, we obeyed her.

"And what's this?" she snapped as she snatched my little bag of candy from my clutch and threw it onto the pile of clothing. I looked around; wasn't anyone going to help me? Pushed into a single file, we were led to another room where piles of clothing and linen were stacked on tables. We each were given a long striped flannel nightgown. Lining up again, we were ushered to a long dormitory room where dozens of cots were lined side by side.

"You here! You there!" she ordered. "Now everyone get undressed and get into bed. No talking and no crying," she snapped. Confused, I did as the others were doing. Too scared to cry and bewildered almost to numbness, I whispered softly, "Where is someone? Helene? Be Boos? Mama?" I cried as a deep hurt engulfed me completely.

The matron walked briskly toward the door, turned sharply, and glanced over at all of us. Apparently satisfied, she reached up, and suddenly, we were plunged into total darkness.

Sobs and sniffles were heard throughout the large room. Instantly the lights came on again. Most of us were sitting up. I glanced toward the door and saw her standing there again, as strange as before. She walked briskly between the cots and started turning heads, one this way and one that way. Finished, she stomped back toward the door, eyed all of us a moment, and with a stern and halting tone, said, "I want all of you to shut up!" Slowly I slid under the covers to hide the fear and the tears. Quickly the lights went out.

I lay there, trying to control my sobbing. I kept thinking about Helene and Be Boos. Where were they? I didn't know when I fell asleep, but was I abruptly awakened by a loud, clanging sound. I sat up as did the rest of the kids. There she was again, just as big and ugly as last night. A sudden scary feeling flowed through my whole body.

"Up! Up! Everyone stand at the foot of your bed!" she yelled. I glanced at the little girl next to me and followed her movements. "Now," the woman snapped, "line up single file and follow me. Hurry it up, come on, come on," she ordered. We followed her through several rooms and hallways then down stairways into the basement. Older girls were busy fitting clothes for everyone. We were each given a pair of high-top boots with buttons on them, a pair of long black cotton stockings, puffy large striped bloomers with elastic bands, and a plain light-blue dress. We were told to shower quickly and get dressed by ourselves. Lining up again, towels were thrown around our necks. Several older girls proceeded to give each of us a haircut. Holding my chin, the girl hastily snipped here and there, turning me around to snip more, and then yelled, "Next!" Each of us was given the same square haircut.

The matron continued to give us orders. I didn't like looking at her, so I looked down at the floor. Quickly, her hand was on my chin, pushing my face upward. "You look me in the eyes when I'm talking," she snapped as she pointed into her big green eyes. I felt I was looking into the eyes of a cat. "We will march to the mess hall for breakfast!" she ordered. I noticed groups of children marching in and some groups marching out. I hated everything so far. How strange this place was.

Once inside the large dining room, another leader of sorts led us to our assigned tables. Each table seated three girls and three boys. An older boy and girl stood at each end. We were to stand erect behind our stools, arms at our sides.

Another loud clang was heard. The tall girl told us to pull our stool out and sit up straight. Another loud ring and we were then ordered to start eating. I sat there staring at my plate. To the side of my plate was a large tin cup filled with milk. I never was able to drink milk, and Mama never forced me. And now this one was looking at me, saying, "Drink your milk."

The other girls obeyed her, but I didn't. "Drink it," she ordered me. Lips quivering, I took the cup and brought it to my lips. I couldn't drink it; I wanted to get sick. "Drink it," she ordered again. I hesitated, and she was immediately at my side and lifted the cup to my lips. I pushed it away only to spill half on the table.

"You're not leaving until you drink your milk," she flatly stated. I stared up at her as she was big and different too. Fearfully, I took the cup and forced myself to drink the milk. Tears rolled down my cheeks to slowly mix with the milk.

Satisfied, she sat down again. Oh, how I wanted my sisters. Lifting myself a little, I stared at the many faces, hoping to catch a glimpse of them. "Sit still," the tall girl ordered me. Suddenly, we heard the loud ringing sound again. We were told to stand behind our stools. Another ringing sound was made, and we were led single file again out of the mess hall.

Once outside, an elated feeling seemed to flow within me. I felt a certain presence as I glanced at the sky. It was here; the sun was here! So big and shining and warm. *It followed me,* I thought. *It came along with me, our best friend, Tommy's and mine!*

A harsh voice interrupted my happiness. "Move along quickly," said the matron as we were forced to march toward the girls' dormitory and down into the basement, where my friend was no more.

Once inside, we were separated into companies according to grades. I was starting kindergarten, so I was put into Company F. There were at least twenty of us in this group. The tall matron did a lot of talking, much of which I didn't understand. We were then led to a dark large room. Lights suddenly went on, and I noticed a long table covered with white sheets. A large pan was filled with kerosene and large tin lizzie combs. Some older girls came into the room to stand behind the tables and proceeded to douse our hair with kerosene. Large towels were wrapped around our heads, and we were told to sit on the floor against the wall.

I knew what kerosene was as Papa used a little to start the fire to warm our house and also to put into the lamps we used for light. Never was it used on my head. I started to cry. *Why are they doing this?* I thought. Mama always warned us never to touch the kerosene; only Papa could, and here were strangers soaking our heads.

I sat on the floor along the wall and felt the kerosene covering my face and neck. This was their torturous method for all newcomers to go through. A procedure used as a precaution to kill head lice. Some of the girls were being smeared with an awful-smelling thick brown salve. By this time, we were all very much confused once more. Silent tears were falling, only to be unanswered.

A short time later, Company F was led upstairs to where the beds were. An officer showed us how to properly make a bed. Tight sheets and square corners were ordered. We were also told how to fold our nightgown neatly and to place it at the foot of the bed. She then brought us into the washroom, where we were taught the proper use of the facilities, as well as brushing our teeth properly. We were then led to a smaller room where in the center was a low-lying brown leather cot. "This is where we bring you when you disobey any rules. And these," she continued as she took a wide leather strap and wooden paddle off the wall, "are what we use to spank you!" I stared at the huge paddle, at the strap, and at the cot. I vaguely understood what she meant, yet I knew she was projecting something scary and mean. The entire room became silent, anxiety mounting, everyone wanting to leave this room.

In a short while, all companies were once lined up in the large room. The main matron was walking quickly, eyeing each and every company. My eyes followed her movements. Suddenly, I caught sight of my sister Be Boos across the room. "Be Boos!" I yelled and ran to her side, holding on to her.

Just as quick, an officer grabbed me. "Get back to your company," she ordered. Resisting her, I pushed and tried holding out my hand so I could touch my sister. Roughly I was pushed back into line again.

The tall matron walked up to me. Holding my chin up very firmly, she said, "I don't want to hear that, that Indian talk again. Understood!" I could barely see her face through my watery eyes. It was the last time I saw my sister for many days.

# ATTENTION! RIGHT FACE!

Just imagine if you will: children aged five, six, and seven marching around like little soldiers. Forced to learn various drills that were complicated, especially so when you didn't understand most of the language being used to instruct you. And so it was on that following morning, Company F was taken out on the square to learn the various drills of marching.

The officer stood in front of us and yelled, "Everyone stand erect and face me! Now, when I say *right face*, turn your right foot like this and turn right. When I say *left face*, turn your left foot like so and turn left. When I say *turn about-face*, put your right foot back on your toes and turn around. Now we will practice these turns until you get them right. Everyone ready? Right face!" she yelled. As you can imagine, little feet started scuffling in every direction. "No! No! No!" she screamed at us. "Attention," she snapped. Startled, we all fell into line again as she stood there with the most disgusting look on her face.

By this time, there were several companies drilling around the square. I glanced around, scanning with my eyes, trying so hard to see my sisters. The girls were unrecognizable as all dressed and looked alike.

A huge lump formed in my throat as tears welled up in my eyes. *Where are they?* I thought. Taking me back to reality, the officer yelled again, "That's enough for the day! You will go back to the dorm and prepare for dinner. Double-time, run!" she ordered as we all started running in unison. "One-two, one-two, one-two . . ."

It was the first of many practices. Little did we know we would be forced to get up at six o'clock in the morning to practice these drills before breakfast, which was not to our liking. All those rights and lefts were getting me confused. Yet eventually, we mastered the daily routine almost to perfection.

# UNKNOWN EXPECTATIONS

How do you forget the world you were born into? How do you forget your parents, your lifestyle, your language, and most importantly, the love and freedom and simplicity of life? All these to be snatched away from you at five years old, and then to suddenly be forced to do a turn about-face into a world of unknown expectations.

I was constantly observing, imitating, and trying to find the answers to this very complicated world. The numerous rules and orders that had to be obeyed, the constant loud, shrill tones of voices in command, the strict reminder, "Do not speak your Indian language." The bewilderment of not knowing right from wrong left me completely in a constant daze. And in spite of all the differences in the emotionalism of my being, somewhere in the darkest corner of my knowing, I sensed that this power that surrounded me was stronger and more powerful that what I had ever known before.

There is knowledge to be found within the framework of the unknown, and slowly the changes came. Each dawn would bring another day of time, and then the darkness that found me trying to find the answers that I knew were there within my reach. I was trying desperately to accept this change, yet the echo of the yesterdays kept mixing with my present thoughts.

Unknowingly, I was drawn into a state of withdrawal. An awful fear possessed me. I shied away from all who came close to me. Gone was the desire to see my sisters. I felt resentment because of their absence. I refused to talk, eat, or play. I didn't cry easily anymore. All I wanted now was to be alone.

While the other kids were at play, I would find my own secluded spot somewhere and sit on the ground to look at the sun, my friend. I remember its warmth. I wanted to reach out to it; there was always that distance.

At night when most were asleep, I was wide-awake. I could hear the squeaking of the chains from the swings or the sound of a distant car. Creeping quietly out of bed, I would make my way to the long, slim window to look at the dark night. Somewhere in the distance was the faint, lonesome sound of a train whistle. I wanted to be where it was. Maybe it would take me home again. My throat would start to hurt, and a dull feeling of hopelessness would overcome me as I made my way back to my bed.

More changes occurred that even I didn't realize was happening to my physical being. I was told to report to the matron's office each morning and evening to drink extra milk. The matron would stand me on her desk and hand me a bottle of milk that seemed to get bigger every day.

"You have to drink extra milk and eat extra lunches," she stated. I was bewildered.

I stared at the bottle and at her and cried, "I don't like milk!"

"Drink it!" she demanded. I turned away quickly. "You will stay here until you drink it all," she ordered.

I cried more and proceeded to sip the milk. I started to gag and tried to push it away from my mouth. "Drink it or I will have to use this," she warned as she held up the wooden ruler. Too scared to retaliate any longer, I started to swallow the milk. I felt I was going to burst open, which was what I did. Up came the milk through my nose and through my mouth. I started to scream and cry louder and then started to urinate on her desk. I could not hold back anything. My frustrations were too forceful.

"I want my sisters," I cried. Disgusted, she told an officer to get my sisters.

The matron scolded me and sternly said, "Do not let this happen again!" I glanced up and saw Be Boos running toward me.

"Be Boos," I cried. She put her arm around me and, in our native language, told me not to cry.

"She might hit you, so stop crying," she whispered in my ear. "Drink the milk, then she will let you go," she went on. I stared at the huge bottle again.

"It's too much, and it will make me throw up again," I cried further.

Holding me, Be Boos whispered again, "Drink it, my sister, I didn't like it either, but now I drink it." Be Boos told me I was not drinking milk and not eating enough food. "You'll get sick, you might die. You have to do this all the time until you get well. Look at your legs and your arms! You're like a little bird! Mama will cry when she sees you. Is this what you want, for Mama to cry?" I took the milk and drank it. I did not want my mama to cry.

And so the days passed, and the changes slowly came to settle within me, to be embedded with the time. Gone were the vivid pictures of my parents, sisters, and brothers. Only a blurred vision of what used to be existed in my mind. Desperately, I tried to cling to the faded past, which was slowly being erased from my mind. Now only certain incidents would bring on loneliness, and just as quickly, the feeling was gone.

# KINDERGARTEN

The days sped by. School had started, and I had the most wonderful person for a teacher. She was tall and slim and had the kindest voice that I had heard since leaving home.

Our classroom was filled with all kinds of mind snatchers imaginable to seduce a child's curious mind. On one side of the room were shelves stacked with storybooks that captured my wonderment. This was where I sat on the floor and turned page after page of unknown fascination. For a while, at least my sorrows would disappear. My curiosity would race along, taking me into an utopia of wonders. For a while, it was a comforting detour from the now that I was in.

It was here that I first became aware of the various holidays. Halloween came around, and all the black cats, witches, and mask making did not have too much appeal for me. It didn't seem to have any connection to the happiness that I needed. The events concerning Thanksgiving were more softening to my heart. Our teacher began teaching us the song lyrics "Over the river and through the woods to grandfather's house we go . . ." This made me feel like we were singing about home and family and of a huge feast to thank God for the land of the plenty.

We had this Thanksgiving feast with many strange foods that I had never tasted before. I remember eyeing my overloaded plate piled high and felt I would surely get sick to my stomach, thinking I would have to eat it all. I sat there nibbling at the food, and all the while, I was trying to think of a way to dispose of it. I glanced at my middy blouse and dark-blue pleated skirt that each of us was told to wear for this occasion. I didn't see any pockets to hide my food in, although what I did notice were the puffy big bloomers that were showing under my skirt.

"Eat all your food," said the leader of our table. I picked up the celery stick, brought it to my mouth, and sensed immediately that I couldn't eat it. Quickly I brought it down to my lap. Easing my pleated skirt upward, I lifted the elastic band circling my knee and pushed the stick of celery out of sight. Very cautiously, I slipped more food below the table then into my secret hiding place. Fortunately, I was not caught. I was to use this sneaky method of disposal many times in the coming months.

# CHRISTMAS

Thanksgiving had passed, and now our teacher was talking to us about another holiday, CHRISTMAS!

Up went pictures of a smiley, fat little man all dressed in red, with little red bells dangling up above, along with paper streamers. The teacher read stories about Santa and his little reindeer and the promise that Santa was going to bring each of us a surprise gift and lots of candy and nuts. "But you must be good children," she warned us. I wanted to be good as I was so anxious to see this fat little man who was called Santa Claus.

With all this excitement, sudden instincts would surface, and I would keep my mind on happy things to come. I was feeling different, thinking differently; apparently, I was being conquered. Whatever the cause, I began to be more outward, more expressive, and more talkative. I began to enjoy myself. The hours I spent in kindergarten class were by far the happiest. It was one attraction after another. Every incident caught my interest. I began to be a part of the group.

And so it was, each holiday brought along anticipation and excitement filled with added happiness.

# FIRST YEAR ENDING

Spring was in the air, and there was much talk of going home for the summer. My gladness joined that of the others in the youthful glee. Many times, especially when the lights were out, I would lie in bed wide-awake and try to envision my home, my family. It always seemed like I was looking through a frosted window. No matter what the case may be, I knew in my heart they were for real, and I would know and see them soon.

As the time for our departure drew near, one by one my friends were receiving word of when their parents or relatives would come and take them home.

*When are Papa and Mama coming?* I thought. One evening after supper, Helene found me while at play.

"We got a letter from Mama. We're not going home this summer," she said bluntly. "But guess what? Mama sent us some money, ten cents. We can get ten suckers or ten sticks of rainbow gum. The matron said I can have the money Saturday morning."

I was elated; my own rainbow bubble gum! For now, my mind focused on the happy moments to come.

Saturday morning came, and my sister gave me three suckers and three long sticks of colored bubble gum. I ran to where my friends were to show off my goodies. They stood around me, waiting for the unwrapping. Slowly I slid the paper off the beautiful red sucker. I gave it one little lick and covered it again with the wrapper.

"Let's leave her, she just wants to make us wish," someone said as they ran away toward the swings. I remembered feeling very sad. I had my candy and my bubble gum, but I didn't have my friends. That incident made me realize that having nothing was better than the candy.

That evening stretched into a summer of friendless days. Gone were friends, teachers, and others. There were only a few of us left to spend the summer at school. The rules were more relaxed, so we were given more privileges than before. I remember going downtown to watch silent movies, a first for many of us. I enjoyed watching Charlie Chaplin and those funny little boys on the Rascals and the Gang even though I didn't know how to read yet.

We all ate breakfast at the dining hall, but we were given sack lunches for dinner and supper. It was fun sitting on the lawn, each with a brown paper sack filled with sandwiches wrapped in newspaper.

In spite of all these extras, I missed my friends very much. I was anxious for school to start again.

# PART TWO

# MY SECOND YEAR AWAY

Little Indian, Sioux or Crow . . .

Little frosty Eskimo.

Little Turk or Japanese,

Oh, don't you wish that you were me?

I was to ponder this last sentence for many days.

The first year passed, and the second year was dawning, opening another year of new experiences. Familiar faces returned; new faces appeared, which brought along some excitement that made past sorrows somehow distinct.

I was now in the first grade. My teacher was an old redhead. She was short, stocky, and very stern. Unlike in kindergarten, we were instructed and oriented toward the white man's world.

Each morning, we would stand very erect behind our desk and wait for our teacher to make her grand entrance. In unison, we would recite what she had instructed us to say. "Good morning, lovely teacher!" And with that said, she managed to give a quick, false smile. She wasn't lovely at all; she constantly puckered and drooled out of her thick red lips, which made me dislike her immensely.

After reciting the Pledge of Allegiance, we would sing, "America . . . My country 'tis . . . my country . . . Sweet land of liberty . . . Let freedom ring . . ."

It was to be a few years longer before I would fully comprehend this song, "America," but for now, I believed our teacher. After all, she was the instructor, and weren't we being structured?

# STRANGE DIFFERENCES

I had never heard the word *segregation* before, much less knew some meaning pertained to it, yet I sensed that something was happening. Something that was totally different from my natural way of life as I had once known before. Maybe my early upbringing at home, which was indelibly embedded within me, was sending me signals against this newly acquired lifestyle. In some instances, my mind was stubborn to accept; at times, my curious mind would win over, and my thoughts would be in battle as to which one I should accept. I would then want to find out more and more.

Finding out that people had different skin colors, hair, and eyes was one difference that fully disturbed me. All these people around you, especially those with authority, with their white skin and light-colored hair, made me feel inferior. It felt that because of their authority, they were superior in every respect. I also noticed that the children who also had these differences were, in my estimation, more privileged, more noticeable, and received more favors. It also seemed that they had a better knowledge of the English language, more so than the majority of us who were endowed with the brown skin tone I had. I especially noticed these differences in Emma, my best friend. Was this why I wanted Emma for a friend? Was this why I wanted to be like Emma? To be accepted like she was?

I didn't fully comprehend these differences at the time, yet I remember grabbing every chance I had, curious to know the reason, and anxious to find the answers, which most of the time turned out to be a painful disappointment.

And so time passed by.

# AM I LIKE A CROW?

One day, our teacher divided us into four groups: the Canaries, Robins, Bluebirds, and the Crows. I was placed in the Crows. There were four of us in this group. Large posters depicting the color and size of the birds were hung in front of each row. My friend Emma was a Canary. Such a beautiful small yellow bird. I wanted to be one too, so I raised my hand and asked why I couldn't be a canary also.

"Whenever you learn to speak English better, I may put you there!" the teacher answered. What did she mean? I felt I was learning English very rapidly. Walking up to me, she continued, "You still cannot pronounce the *th* sounds or pronounce your name correctly." I didn't like her. Besides, she looked worse than a crow to me. She looked like a big, fat red rooster, and I wanted to tell her so.

True, my repertoire of the English language was limited. Now, more than ever, I was determined to be a Canary in as short a while as possible. As expected among all children, there was a lot of teasing within the classroom and outside the school grounds. I was teased about being dumb and dark like a crow. I hated first grade. I hated the fact that I couldn't speak English very well. I raved on and on to my friend Emma. There was within me a new awakening of differences.

One day, I asked her, "How come you have red hair? Why is your skin so light and mine is so dark?"

As days passed, she whispered to me one evening. "You have to know my secret, but you can't ever, ever tell anyone," she warned.

"I won't, honest to God," I answered with anxiety.

"If you tell anyone, you will be a big black crow until you're an old lady," she emphasized strongly.

"I promise! Cross my heart!" I answered excitedly.

"Okay, now on Saturday morning after we pick up the papers on the lawn, we will go to the cornfield. We will have to bring water 'cause I need that. Then I'll . . . I can't tell you the rest . . . 'cause that's my secret," she quickly said.

"Will I get white skin?" I anxiously asked.

"White like mine!" she proudly replied. I was so anxious for Saturday to come.

The anticipated day arrived, and after doing our detail work, Emma and I raced to the cornfield. And there, amid the tall cornstalks, Emma proceeded to do her secret. "Now!" she exclaimed. "First, I have to make a little pile of dirt." So we got on our hands and knees and pushed the black dirt into a little pile. "Now you have to pour . . . Oh! OH!" she said as she covered her mouth with her hands.

"What?" I asked.

"We have no water, and we need water," she said, hopeless.

"I know what! Should we? You know," I sheepishly asked.

"All right, you first. I won't look," she said. So I did my thing, and then it was Emma's turn. Getting down on our knees again, Emma mixed it with her hands. "Now, it's ready!" said Emma as she proceeded to plaster the mud on my face, neck, arms, and legs.

We sat there waiting because Emma said the mud had to dry. She would look at me and start to giggle. "You look so funny." She giggled.

"You look just like our teacher," I retorted. "You have red hair and freckles just like her. She looks just like Little Red Hen. Do you like her?"

"Sometimes," she answered. "Do you like her?"

"Well, she's kind of like a bird, she's got feathers on her neck," I told her.

Emma started to giggle. "You're funny, I won't tell her what you said 'cause she'll get mad." Then I wondered, was Emma going to tell the teacher? I started thinking how at times Emma was kind of a tattletale. What if she did tell the teacher? I sat there worried. I didn't trust Emma right then, yet so many times before, I did.

Having lost track of time, we were suddenly startled by the sound of bells ringing. We knew it meant it was time to line up to prepare for dinner. "OH! OH!" Emma said as she scrambled to her feet and quickly started to run toward the dormitory.

"Emma, wait for me," I hollered. I stood up and glanced at my arms, my legs. Desperately, I tried to scratch the mud off. What was I going to do? I didn't know. There was only one thing to do: just follow Emma.

Up ahead, I could see the companies all lined up in front of the building. As I ran and got closer, trying to catch Emma, I noticed some heads turning and then the sound of laughter. I raced right up to my position and stood there out of breath. The officer came up to me and, pushing my chin upward, said, "And where were you? You will be punished! Edna, take this little mud ball down to the shower room. Move!" ordered the second officer. As Edna led me away, I could still hear the snickering and laughter behind me. Edna directed me to the shower room. She told me to hurry up. She didn't have to tell me; I pulled off my clothes as fast as I could. At last, I was going to have white skin like Emma's! I stood there in the dark cement stall and let the water whisk away the black mud, anxious to see the results.

"That's enough, get out now," the officer ordered. Excitedly, I stepped out. I held out my arms toward the glare of the light to look at my white skin. All I saw was wet brown skin staring back at me. I wanted to cry. I stooped down to look at my legs, no difference there either. She lied!

"Emma lied to me," I silently sobbed to myself.

I was full of frustration as I followed Edna back to the company line. Once there, I was told to go to bed without supper. I remember not caring about missing meals; it was the thought of being alone that I dreaded.

# I WAS BEING RE-CREATED!

As young as I was, I sensed that there was a certain direction of thought, mannerism, and stimulation that was being pushed into us at school. Young at heart, we all accepted this as a normal process to be recognized and to be learned. Each day within the classroom, we were exposed to various world cultures and lifestyles of other people. I didn't know who I was at the time, so my curiosity raced along. I wanted to be like so many others. At first, to be like a little Japanese girl held my fancy. The lovely kimonos and dainty little colored fans. And the song that goes like this:

I came from the land of Japan . . . Of Japan

With parasol and with fan . . . and with fan . . .

I live across the rolling sea . . .

*That's it,* I thought. *But I don't want to live across the rolling sea.* Did I want to be a little African girl? No, I thought. The teacher told us that they stuck sticks and bones in their ears and nose, and the pictures of these people put some fear into me too. Did I want to be an Indian? After looking at the pictures of the Indians on the warpath, fighting, scalping women and children, and oh, with such ugly faces, *No! Indians are mean people, I'm glad I'm not an Indian,* I thought.

For a while, the little Dutch girl amid the lovely tulip gardens held my childish interest, but her wooden shoes would hurt my already deformed feet. Feet that had an everlasting hurt from wearing stiff, hard leather high-tops, which constantly left my feet covered with blisters and calluses. I knew who I wanted to be: like Sally in our primer books. The loving mother and father, the nice house, riding a bicycle, roller-skating, pretty little dresses. She was everything I wanted to be.

# A NEW FRIEND

An incident happened that seemed to induce my desire to be like Sally.

One evening after supper, while on the playground, a little blond girl came riding by on her bicycle. She stopped and asked if anyone wanted a ride on her bike. Being closer to her than the others were, I quickly answered, "I will!"

"Come on!" she said. Quickly I ran up to her. Showing me where to sit, she pedaled off up the road and back again. What a glorious feeling, my first ride on a bicycle.

"What's your name?" she asked.

"Metha," I answered.

"Metha? I never heard that name before!"

"What's your name?" I asked her.

"Barbara," she replied. Then we rode on and on, talking and giggling. Such fun we had.

"Shall I come back tomorrow?" she asked.

"Yes," I answered anxiously.

"All right, but I gotta go now," she said. I stood there and watched as she rode away.

This was the first of Barbara's many trips back to the school. We became very close friends, and Barbara always kept her promise. The days that she didn't come to see me made me very sad. I would stand at the curb and longingly watch the road toward town, hoping she would come.

It was on a Saturday afternoon that I first defied the rules of the school. Barbara came and asked if I wanted to go uptown with her. "Sure," I answered. Besides, I didn't like the silly little rules at school anyway. What if I did get punished? I didn't care.

Barbara pedaled her bike right up to the main street in front of the drugstore. "Come, I have to see my dad," she told me.

I followed Barbara into the store. "Daddy, this is my friend, Metha!" she told a man standing behind the counter. The man looked at me and gave a friendly smile.

"So you're the little girl from the boarding school Barbara talks about."

Barbara then asked her dad for two quarters so we could go to the movies. As she pedaled to the theater, Barbara told me her dad owned the drugstore and her mom worked every day. She was the only child, and she was glad I was her friend. She also told me that the movie we were going to see was about ballet dancing.

"Ballerina?" I asked.

"You know, toe dancing," she said. No, I didn't know; I had never heard such a word before. The movie was captivating. Such a graceful little girl swaying, dipping, whirling on her little toes. She reminded me of a beautiful butterfly. I wanted to see the movie over and over.

Barbara brought me back to the school just as the companies were marching toward the dining hall for supper.

"See ya later!" she said as she turned her bike to ride back to town. I knew I was in deep trouble. As I was running to catch up with my company, someone yelled out my name. I stopped and turned to see the head matron briskly walking toward me.

"And who gave you permission to leave the school grounds?" she loudly asked. "Go to my office this minute!" Once inside the office, the matron reminded me about the school rules. "You are punished, and you will go to bed without supper. And you will have to tell your little friend that she can't be coming here to pick you up whenever she wants. Now go straight to your bed, and don't move out of it!"

Being alone in the empty big dormitory brought on streaks of self-pity, but it was quickly erased from my mind when I thought about the exciting afternoon I had spent with Barbara. With more than enough solitude surrounding me, I did some deep thinking. As usual, my imagination sprouted roots of self-exaltation. Quickly, I got out of my bed to do what my mind was illuminating. Up and down the aisle I danced, swaying, spinning, and jumping. I stopped to evaluate my performance. A small cloud of disappointment began to shadow my enthusiasm. My body wasn't keeping in tune with my mind. *But I want to be a dancer,* I thought. Quickly, my mind was rejuvenated. I was now determined to carry on my childish desires. I would think of something soon.

When she finally did come to the school to see me, it was with much sorrow, when I had to tell her that she could not visit me anymore. She didn't understand why, and neither could I.

U. S. GOVERNMENT INDIAN SCHOOL, WAHPETON, N. D.

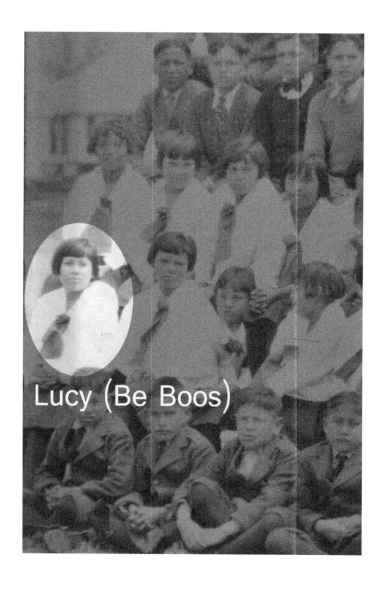

Helene

Metha at age 16

Metha and husband, John
September 19, 1941

# MY FIRST ACCOMPLISHMENT

Loneliness has a way of quietly fading from a young child's heart. For me, it was the thought of being a ballerina just like the little girl in the silent movie. Now instead of playing hopscotch or playing on the swings, I would sneak away from my friends and go down into the basement of the girls' dormitory.

After taking off my clumsy stogie shoes and stuffing the bottom of my dress under my bloomers, I would try standing on the tips of my toes. It seemed so easy watching the little girl in the movie. I would try and try again. Something was wrong; I couldn't do it. I sat and examined my feet. They were ugly. They were scarred, and they seemed awfully big. They were not dainty like the little dancer's. And then I noticed that my arms were too long and bony. How rounded and graceful were the dancer's. With all these thoughts, I disappointed myself. Yet the little dance routine and the little song, which consisted of la-la-la-la-las, kept springing around in my head.

Suddenly, I had an idea. Although this was only my secret, I knew that now, I had to let my friends know about it. I needed one of them to be the little ballerina dancer. I ran back to the playground, where my friends were. I knew that all I had to do to draw their attention was to sing a little con song I had learned from others.

I sang, "I have a secret, you don't know . . . I have a secret, you don't know . . ."

As expected, curiosity got the best of them.

"What's your secret?" they asked.

"You promise not to tell?" I said.

"Cross my heart and hope to die," they chorused.

I noticed that Marie, the quiet one, was standing off to the side. Marie, it seemed, always needed a little nudge or a special invitation. "Marie, you can come too," I said.

Finding a spot away from the others, we sat in a circle on the ground. First, I told them about Barbara. I told them about the silent movie we went to and about the beautiful little dancer. I told them how Barbara got to see real-life dancers in town and how they were so pretty in their little dresses. I also told them that Barbara said that anyone could be a dancer like that if you really wanted to be one. And now, I wanted to be that dancer. But my feet hurt, I had blisters, and I just wanted someone else to be the dancer.

"I can dance on my toes! I can dance on my toes, see!" they all boasted. I told them we would go to the basement, where no one would see us.

Once there, off went the stogie shoes; up went the dresses to be stuffed under the bloomers legs. I then showed them the little routine I had made up.

One by one, they all tried. They were awful, very clumsy, and ungraceful. I didn't like what I saw. And Marie, who hadn't bothered to join, was sitting and watching us.

"Come on, Marie, you try," I prodded.

With a little more coaxing, she took her stogies off and said, "I know the dance, I've been watching." She balanced on the tips of her toes and started to twirl around and around. She too reminded me of a little butterfly.

"Marie, you will be the dancer!" I told her excitedly.

I remember the many hours Marie and I spent practicing our little routine. She danced with her feet, and I danced with my hands, giving motions of what I wanted her to do. Our music was composed of many more la-la-la-la-las. Choppy la-las meant certain movements.

Marie was perfect for the dancing role. It was an exciting time. I kept telling Marie that she was a better dancer than the little girl in the movie. To me, she was the greatest, and that was all she needed. A little nudge, a little push, and she was completely lost in her dancing.

Unexpectedly, the great show-off day arrived. As we were leaving the dining hall one evening, it started to rain in torrents. Because of this, we were led to the basement to spend the entire evening. It was like a severe punishment to have to spend time inside. Longingly we stood on hard cement benches to stare out the musty windows, hoping for the sun to shine.

We tried playing all kinds of simple little games, which were quite boring and were quickly placed aside for something more exciting.

"Marie, shall we do our dance?" I whispered to her.

"I don't care," she replied.

I remember running to the middle of the room and telling everyone that Marie and I were going to do a little ballerina dance. But I raved on, "You all have to sit down very quietly, and when Marie takes her bow, everybody will clap their hands."

There were at least thirty or forty children in the room. Immediately, they scampered to sit on the benches. Helping Marie stuff her dress up into her bloomer legs and making sure she remembered to bow at the end, we were ready.

I went to sit on the center of one of the cement benches. I gave Marie her cue. "Dum-dum-dum." Marie perched on her toes, her arms up above her head, forming an arch. And then I let out with the la-la-las. It was perfect! No mistakes!

Marie took her bow as clapping and yelling broke out. "Marie, dance again! Dance again!" they shouted.

We did another performance with the same enthusiasm. They gathered around Marie, telling her how good she was. I remember sitting alone, looking on with a happy feeling, sharing the enthusiasm, and knowing I had done what Barbara had said, "Anyone can be a dancer!"

# WHY IS YOUR NAME LIKE A BIRD'S?

Every incident that happened at this Indian boarding school was particularly interesting to me as there was always a sense of curiosity. I wanted answers to everything. I remember very distinctly one day in the classroom, the subject being discussed was about how people and places got their names.

After some time, our teacher mentioned to us that there was a reason why our names were different. I glanced at others and wondered why some of the kids had names like Eagle, Yellow Bird, Black Bear. And then I wondered about my name. What did it mean? I could not find an answer. It was so different from most of the other kids'.

Some evenings as we sat around on the playground, I would ask some little girls how they got their names. One little girl told me her name was Running Horse because they had a horse. I recalled wishing I had a beautiful name like the others had. To me, their names were about real, living things, and mine didn't mean anything. I wanted so much to have a bird name like some of my friends had.

# LITTLE OLD LADY AND THE PARROT

One Sunday morning, we attended mass as usual at Saint John's Catholic Church. For some reason, our leader led us on a street different from the usual. It was in the springtime, and I was eagerly enjoying the beauty and scenery before me. As we turned the block, I noticed a pretty little white house with a red roof, shutters, and doors. A white picket fence surrounded it with a fancy wrought-iron gate. On the porch, a white-haired little old lady was rocking in a chair. Walking slowly, I let the others pass me by. I lingered a little to stare at the beautiful, colored tulips near the fence. Suddenly, I heard a cackling sound from above. I looked up and saw a wire cage with the most beautiful bird inside that was hanging from a branch.

Glancing toward the porch, I saw the little old lady coming toward me. She was wearing a long dress and a little white apron. She was smiling as she came close to me.

"Do you like my parrot?" she asked. "My Polly talks, come, Polly, talk for the little girl. Say 'Polly wants a cracker.'"

"Polly wants a cracker!" answered the bird. I stared at the bird, at the old lady; it was so hard to believe what just happened. How could she make a bird talk? Turning quickly, I ran to catch up with the group.

I told my friends what I just saw, which left them just as excited as I was. We anxiously waited for the following Sunday. And so it was that we eagerly looked forward for Sundays to roll around. We enjoyed talking to Polly and the little old lady.

Then one Sunday after Mass, our leader decided to take the former route back to the school. As the group walked along, my friend and I sneaked across the street to the next block, where the parrot lived. Hastily we ran up to the picket fence.

I noticed the absence of the old lady and Polly. The doors and shutters were all closed, and her little rocking chair was gone. There was an awful stillness all around although the beautiful, colored tulips were still swaying slightly.

"Let's go," my friend said as she ran down the block. I couldn't leave, not just then; I wanted to see Polly and the little old lady.

"Little old lady," I called and called again. There was no answer. Heartbroken, I turned away, not caring what would happen next. Somewhere in the far distance, I knew I had once known a little old lady, but where?

# TIME KEPT PASSING

Time has passed, and I had completely forgotten about Polly, the parrot. On one Saturday morning while playing on the swings, a shiny big black car drove up to the curb. An elderly, well-dressed woman got off and walked partway to ask directions to a certain building.

Two girls ran up to where she was, and I watched my friends as they talked and giggled with this stranger. Being very cautious but curious, I too ran to join the crowd. "Any what is your name?" I heard her ask one.

"Mary Yellow Hawk," replied the little girl.

"Oh! What a beautiful name!" she exclaimed.

"Any what is your name?" she asked another girl.

"Beulah Black Bear," replied the little girl.

"Any yours?" she asked me.

"Metha," I said, hesitating a little.

"Metha? And what is your last name?"

I didn't want the others to hear me, so I stepped closer to the lady and softly whispered, "Parrot."

"Parrot? Well, that's beautiful too!" she kindly said.

My friends started to giggle. "That's not her name," they shouted, and giggled some more.

Knowing I had done something wrong, I turned and ran quickly back to the swings. I didn't like my friends for the rest of the day.

# TEN MORE DAYS AND I'LL BE FREE!

The second year was coming to a close, and the month of May was waiting to be reborn. There was excitement because of the summer vacation for those who were fortunate to leave. As each day passed, there was a little song some were singing that went this way:

Ten more days and I'll be free . . . from this school of misery.

No more eating government beans, no more sitting on a three-legged stool.

Then they continued with the countdown.

Nine more days . . .

The last three days of school were filled with excitement as each one packed their belongings and talked about their loved ones they would be seeing. Up went the list of those who would be leaving. I didn't try to find out if my sisters and I were one of those, and apparently, my sisters didn't seem to be bothered either.

One by one, my friends left for home until there was only Emma and me. And all too soon, her parents arrived, and Emma too was gone.

If there was any knowledge of why my sisters and I were not going home, it was never mentioned. Whatever the cause, we accepted this fact and were obedient to it.

# PART THREE

# THREE-YEAR CIRCLE—
# ALMOST COMPLETE

Summer settled in, and it was mostly a repeat of the summer before. Once again, I was anxious for friends to return. Most of the kids returned, except Emma. No one seemed to know the reason why.

School started, and I felt the loss of my best friend. Emma had told me that she lived in a big city named Minneapolis. I often wondered where it was. *Someday,* I thought, *I will go and find her.*

It was during this third year that my talents started to surface. I was involved in most of the grade school performances because of my dancing and singing abilities. I enjoyed every moment. It was then that I was the happiest.

To be in the grade school singing quartet was the most exciting. Four of us entertaining at many events, getting to go places, and people were telling us how wonderful our singing was.

At first, we wore the traditional school uniforms when we would perform. Then one day, the four of us were taken to the sewing room to be fitted for new dresses. I remember the beautiful colored voile material in pink, yellow, blue, and pale green. I was chosen to wear the pink because of my skin color. Little petticoats were also sewn for us. How beautiful were the dresses when finished. Row upon row of gathered ruffles, I felt so pretty when I tried it on for the last fitting. Then we were taken to town where each of us was fitted for dainty little black leather shoes.

The first time we wore our new outfit was to a performance at Moorhead, Minnesota. Getting all dressed up was so exciting. We were the envy of all the other little girls who stood around to watch us dress up.

We lined up for one last inspection from the matron. She eyed us over, front and back. Then she motioned for me to follow her up to her office. Once there, she stood me atop her desk and went into her private quarters, returning immediately, holding a pretty flowered container.

Opening it, she lifted out a soft large puff and swabbed it on my legs, arms, and face. I remember the smell of it, so nice. Finished, she told me to go back where the others were. I glanced at my arms, and I saw a shiny white film. I sniffed some more, and the smell was wonderful. Then I went to stand by the other girls, hoping they would notice. I wondered why the matron chose me for this nice-smelling stuff. I lifted my arm and sniffed some more so the others would notice me.

One of the girls standing by me asked, "What's on your face and arms?"

"Something from a pretty little box, do you want a smell?" I asked her. They all came closer to examine me, and with a mocking look, they started to whisper and giggle.

"I know why she did that," said one of the girls as they giggled some more.

Just then, the matron came to get us.

It wasn't until much later that I learned why the matron did what she did. *Was my skin too dark to sing?* I thought.

# ONSTAGE

On one occasion, I was asked by my teacher to recite from memory the story of the three bears for a Sunday evening assembly. I was chosen for the part because of my ability to memorize and also because I somehow liked to be a show-off. I remember very plainly my teacher coaching me on how to present myself onstage and how to pronounce certain words, especially those with the *th* sound.

Sunday evening came, and I was anxiously standing behind the curtains with my teacher, waiting for my turn onstage. "Remember now, be sure to pronounce your name correctly like I told you, all right?" she reminded me. I nodded my head. I knew I could do this story almost without thinking. And then, it was my turn. I walked very straight to the middle of the stage.

I clasped my hands behind my back, like my teacher said, and very loudly said, "Hello, my name is M-e-e-th-a."

There was a ripple of laughter in the audience. "My teacher said if I put my tongue up like this, I can say M-e-e-th-a," I repeated. Much laughter broke out, which caused me to be somewhat disturbed. I glanced to the side of the stage and saw my teacher with her hands to the sides of her head.

"Go on, go on. Once upon a," she whispered to me.

I looked back at the audience and proceeded with my story. "Once upon a time, der was tree little bears!" From that moment on, I didn't give a care how words were pronounced. As I could sense by the big grins on the people's faces and the look in their eyes, they liked my performance. I finished my story, did my bow, and ran off to the side where my teacher was standing, knowing I had done a good job. Just then, an elderly lady came up to us. She was very tall and had on a nice silk dress and a pretty hat. She held out her arms to embrace me. Stooping down, she looked me in the eyes and told me she very much enjoyed my story.

As she talked, I noticed the pretty big round glass beads dangling in front of my face. They were deep red in color and the size of marbles. I stood there wishing they were mine. As she oohed and aahed, I heard her saying, "I just have to give you something." I kept my eyes glued on her beads and then lifted my hands to finger them. "You like these beads? You can have them, honey!" She unclipped them and put them in my hand. A glorious happiness engulfed me. I couldn't wait to get back to the girls' basement playroom so I could tear them apart and show off my beautiful red marbles to my friends. Now I wouldn't have to beg or wish for marbles anymore.

# RUNAWAYS

During the course of this third year at school, I became aware of the many runaways that had and still were taking place at the school. Children, whose homes were hundreds of miles away, were desperately trying to find ways to go back to their homeland. Most of the time, the children were caught and were severely punished.

I remember very distinctly on a Saturday morning, our company was detailed to wash and scrub walls and benches in the dormitory basement playroom. One of the girls who were wiping windowsills very excitedly called us to look out the window. Scrambling up the cement benches, I looked out and saw at least a dozen little boys with dresses on parading back and forth in front of our building. Throwing our mops and rags aside, we hurriedly went to watch the boys. Most of the girls were laughing and giggling, finding this to be very funny.

Everyone laughed except for one little girl named Sylvia, who was standing off to one side, crying her heart out. I went to stand by her and asked her why she was crying. She tried to answer me, but her sobbing was too strong. Sylvia was a beautiful little girl. Her skin was as white as milk; her curly dark hair was dangling around her face, which was moist with tears. She was sort of a shy little girl, and although I knew that she was from the same homeland as I was, we seldom played together. "What's the matter?" I asked again.

Sobbing, she said haltingly, "My brother, they're being mean to my brother!"

I stared at the little boys who were once more approaching where we were standing. They did look silly; I too wanted to laugh. Most of the boys seemed very embarrassed as they passed with heads hung. And they didn't try to look at the crowd of girls who were giggling and making remarks as to how cute they looked with dresses on, with the exception of one. This little boy was about ten years old, a very handsome boy with large dark eyes and curly dark hair. Showing a strong look of defiance, he glanced at the girls and snapped his eyes, apparently very insulted for what they were making him do.

"That's my brother there," Sylvia said as she pointed to the curly-headed boy.

"What did they do?" I asked. Still crying, she told me how these boys sneaked away from the boys' dormitory and ran away to go home.

"But they got caught, and now they're being punished!" she cried. I glanced once more at the little boy. *What if he was my brother? I thought.* Little did I know he would be more than a brother in the years ahead.

# GOING HOME

Once again, the month of May rolled around. I seemed to sense that it always brought much joy as well as sorrow. Joy was the happy celebration of May Day, which was filled with all kinds of fun activities that usually lasted all week. Sorrow usually came at the end of the month and in saying farewell.

It was now three years since my sisters and I had said farewell to our parents, and now, we were told that we would be returning home. This time, the farewells would be said to our friends, whom we had accepted as our family during these long years.

It was with mixed feelings that my sisters and I packed our few belongings for our return to home and to family. I, at least, didn't seem to have the eagerness that many of my friends projected. I had been settled here for three long years, and the thought of leaving my second family brought on a loneliness I had once known before.

On the morning of departure, I told my friends that I was going back the following year and for them to be sure to go back also. "Good-bye!" we all joined in saying, and waved as the truck sped toward town where we were to get on the train to head for home.

Riding on the train going home made me ask questions for my sisters. "Are you glad to be going home?" I asked Helene first.

"Well, of course, aren't you?" she asked.

"Lucy, are you glad to be going home too?" I asked.

"I don't know, I guess," she replied. And then I asked if we had a nice house and other things we were used to having at school. "Don't be silly, we must have our little log house yet. Mama and Papa are poor, they don't have nice things like that!"

I felt disappointed. I sat there wondering about lots of things. "I wonder how Mama and Papa looked, and Tommy?" I was trying very hard to picture them, but I couldn't. Most of the ride was spent looking out the train window. At times, my mind would wander back to what I had left behind. And then, it would zigzag back to what expectations lay ahead.

It was getting late in the afternoon as I noticed the sun was in a position to let me know that it was nearing suppertime. I looked around at some of the older girls and noted some excitement as they pressed their faces against the windowpanes too. "There's Rolla," someone shouted. I remember Helene and Lucy showing some excitement too.

"We're almost there," said Lucy. I too looked out the window and saw houses and a couple of tall buildings up ahead.

"That's Rolla," said Helene. "That's the place where we took the train to go to school."

I noticed the train slowing down. I kept my face pressed against the windowpane as we moved at a very slow pace. I also noticed a large group of people standing on a wooden platform up ahead. Getting closer, I could see the people very plainly.

"Mama and Papa must be there! I wonder if we'll know them," said Helene. I was still looking out the window when the train stopped. I stared at the people, people I didn't know.

"Where's Mama and Papa?" I asked Helene.

"They're right over there."

I looked but I didn't recognize anyone. "Where?" I asked.

"See that one in the blue overalls? And Mama, she's got on a black coat." My searching eyes rested on the tall man in blue overalls and the woman in a black coat. She was wearing a little red tam slightly tilted to one side. No recognition surfaced at the moment. They were so very old and so very strange!

*Helene must be making a mistake,* I thought. *That can't be them,* I thought, feeling very confused. Glancing quickly at the crowd, I saw a tall young woman dressed very smartly, standing, waiting for someone. "I think that's Mama there," I said, pointing to the young lady.

Helene, very annoyed, looked at me and said, "Are you getting silly again? That's a white woman. Come on now, we have to get off now." She directed me to the door and had me step out first. I hesitated a moment and looked out over the crowd.

"My baby, my baby girls!" cried the woman in black as she quickly stepped forward to embrace me. "Helene, Be Boos," she cried out and sobbed as she reached out her arms to encircle them too. I looked up at the tall man standing by her. He had a kind smile on his face, and his eyes were clouded with tears.

Holding out his arms, he said to us, "Remember me?"

There was a slight remembrance of something, yet the long, long absence was playing a stronger role in this reunion. I must have been projecting some kind of slight rejection toward Papa and Mama as Helene slyly gave me an authoritative look and snapped her eyes as if to say, "You behave now!" I was well trained to take orders, so I obeyed Helene's silent message.

Papa had hired our neighbor who had an old Model T Ford to take us home. I sat between Papa and the big, heavyset dark man doing the driving. Mama, Helene, and Lucy sat in the backseat. My sisters seemed to be accepting the fact that this was home and family. So I too believed this was the right thing to do.

Arriving at our neighbor's house, the dark man said he was sorry that he couldn't drive any farther as the road was too narrow and bumpy. Papa paid and thanked the man, and off we went on foot through a wooded narrow trail, a distance of about one mile.

So beautiful was the quiet of the woods, only the chirping of the birds and an occasional caw from a crow. Lovely shadows were forming all around us, and the sun was peeking through the thick spring foliage, creating a peacefulness that touched you completely. "Are we almost there?" I asked as a sudden gladness surged through me.

"Almost," said Papa.

"You know, you have two baby brothers that you've never seen," said Mama. "Their names are George and Charlie." Upon hearing that news, it brought me more happiness and anxiousness to get home.

Coming out of the woods, we came upon a clearing on a hill that sloped downward into a valley. There situated amid the soft, rolling hills was a small log cabin. "There's our home, remember it?" said Papa. We stopped to stare as my sisters and I took in the view of the countryside. I noted a few dotted cabins in the distance and a few horses grazing here and there and then the sight of a little boy running and waving his arms, coming toward us.

"That's Tommy," said Mama. "He's supposed to be watching the baby," she laughingly said. Up the hill ran Tommy. As he was coming closer, I noticed he had on patched blue overalls, and he was barefoot. A big, happy smile on his face and out of breath, he ran up to us all. He stopped and stared at us in turns.

"Well, what do you think of your sisters?" Papa asked him.

"Gee, they got big!" he said, still out of breath. He sized us up again and then, very shyly, hugged each of us. "Do you want to see where I chop wood?" he asked us.

"Sure," we all answered as we followed him to the edge of the woods, where he showed us a pile of small sticks he had chopped for Mama. We raced back to where Mama and Papa were descending the hill. "See this flat rock?" he asked me, pointing to a large flat stone half-embedded in the ground. "Remember we used to sit here on this hill?" I tried very hard to bring back those days of long ago, then very slowly, little streaks of remembrance started to push through the haze that had settled over my life for the past three years. I stared at the rock, the scenery around us, the hill we were on; everything looked so different, so much smaller.

"Remember," he said again. Then he giggled and added, "We buried some wild pecan nuts here for the squirrels, but after you left, I took them again." I noticed sadness as he spoke. "But we'll get some more, over there, there's lots of them!" he added. A twinge of happiness surged through me and was to get stronger as we talked childishly. Running again to catch our parents, I saw two little girls at the bottom of the hill, running to meet us too.

"That's Laura and Irene. And those little ones back more are Sonny and George. Let's run," Tommy said as I followed him past Mama and Papa to where my little sisters were. They stood there looking at this stranger, not knowing who I was. Very bashful, they reluctantly accepted the hugs and kisses I gave them. They too seemed like little strangers. On we ran to where Sonny and George were waiting. Sonny had been one year old when we left, and I was seeing my little brother George for the first time.

"Do you know me? I'm your sister," I said. When I tried to kiss them, they shied away and moved to stand behind Tommy. I wanted so much to kiss their little faces.

"Come on, the baby is alone," said Tommy as we ran toward the cabin. There were no detours, no stop signs to hold me back.

"Go! Go!" said my childish heart as I ran following Tommy to the door. I looked inside and saw a wooden box on the floor. Inside was the sweetest little baby I'd ever seen. I remember getting down on the floor and kissing and lifting my little brother. It seemed that I couldn't get enough of him.

Homecoming was so wonderful! Everyone was talking and laughing with a few joyous tears. Eating supper without rules or commands, everyone free and at ease, feeling the love, the closeness. Oh! I just knew that I was having happiness at last! I remember after supper, we went outside to play, romping, laughing, Tommy telling his small experiences and I, mine.

And the darkness came that night; the only lights were the stars, the big round moon, the dim lamp from the cabin window, and the fireflies in the dark. How big, serene, and quiet was the night compared to other nights I had known.

That night, as I lay on my bed on the floor, I glanced at the window and saw many little stars twinkling in the sky, sharing my happiness.

Three long years had passed since my sister Helene had said these words:

> *"TOMORROW, my sister . . .*
> *TOMORROW, we'll go home!"*

And now, that TOMORROW was here at last.

# EPILOGUE

In closing, eighty-two years have passed since I first encountered my Indian boarding school experiences at Wahpeton Indian Boarding School, Wahpeton, North Dakota. I went on to finish high school at Flandreau Indian Vocational High School, Flandreau, South Dakota.

I was eighteen years old, full of aspirations as to my future, when I met for the second time in my life the defiant, curly-headed little boy who had run away from the boarding school as mentioned earlier. We married in the fall of 1941. Ten children were born into our marriage, five boys and five girls. Now I have many lovely grandchildren and great-grandchildren to boast of.

After all these years, my trials and tribulations as a little girl have been reduced to paper. I hope my experiences will give insight to the world what so many young Native Americans endured.

Made in the USA
Coppell, TX
13 December 2021

68393524R00059